W9-AES-537

John F. Kennedy

Catherine Corley Anderson

In Consultation with Martha Cosgrove,
M.A. and Reading Specialist

Lerner Publications Company/Minneapolis

Martha Cosgrove has a master's degree from the University of Minnesota in secondary education, with an emphasis on developmental and remedial reading. She is licensed in 7–12 English and language arts, developmental reading, and remedial reading. She has had several works published, and she gives numerous state and national presentations in her areas of expertise.

Lerner Publications Company
A division of Lerner Publishing Group
241 First Avenue North
Minneapolis, Minnesota 55401 U.S.A.

Website address: www.lernerbooks.com

Library of Congress Cataloging-in-Publication Data

Anderson, Catherine Corley.
    John F. Kennedy / by Catherine Corley Anderson.
        p.   cm. – (Just the facts biographies)
    Includes bibliographical references and index.
    ISBN-13: 978-0-8225-2643-8 (lib. bdg. : alk. paper)
    ISBN-10: 0-8225-2643-3 (lib. bdg. : alk. paper)
    1. Kennedy, John F. (John Fitzgerald), 1917–1963–Juvenile literature.
    2. Presidents–United States–Biography–Juvenile literature. 3. United States–Politics and government–1961–1963–Juvenile literature. I. Title.
    II. Series.
    E842.Z9A63 2006
    973.922'092–dc22   2005007473

Manufactured in the United States of America
1 2 3 4 5 6 – BP – 11 10 09 08 07 06

Contents

CHAPTER 1

GROWING UP RICH

(Above) Jack (right) and Joe Jr. (left) joined their father (center) in Britain on the eve of World War II (1939-1945).

IN THE SUMMER OF **1939**, twenty-two-year-old John F. Kennedy, called Jack by his family, was traveling in Europe. The whole continent seemed to be on the brink of war against Nazi Germany. Jack was gathering information for his father, Joseph P. Kennedy Sr. Joe Sr. was the U.S. ambassador to Great Britain. This meant he represented the U.S.

government in Britain. Jack's job was to give his father views on how people in Europe were feeling and acting during this tense time.

Jack spent several months in Paris, France. He then traveled to eastern Europe, the Soviet Union, Turkey, Palestine, and Belgium. Everywhere he went, he talked to people on the street, as well as to officials at various embassies. Jack finished his trip and went back to London, the capital of Britain, to see his family. Not long after his arrival, Britain declared war against Germany. World War II (1939–1945) had begun.

On September 3, 1939–two days after Britain's declaration of war–a telephone call woke up Ambassador Kennedy in the middle of the night. He was told that a German submarine had torpedoed an unarmed British passenger ship, the *Athenia*. More than three hundred Americans had been aboard. Only some had survived. The ambassador woke up Jack and told him what had happened. Survivors of the attack were being taken to Glasgow, Scotland. He wanted Jack to leave at once for Glasgow to help the American survivors. It was a big job.

When Jack reached Glasgow, he was saddened by the tragedy of so many deaths. He admired the

Survivors of the 1939 *Athenia* tragedy are helped off of the boat that rescued them.

courage of the survivors. And, like them, he was angry at the attack. On the part of his father, the U.S. ambassador, he let the U.S. passengers know that they would be taken to safety on other ships.

Born into a rich family, Jack had never known what it might be like to be poor or in danger. His family had enough money to send him to Harvard University, an expensive school in Massachusetts. But Jack hadn't been studying very hard. He had never faced serious danger from war.

As he watched people coping with an unfair situation, he strongly identified with their anger. He was waking up to the problems of others. It was a

turning point in a life that was to have many
turning points.

EARLY DAYS

John Fitzgerald Kennedy was born on May 29,
1917, to Joseph and Rose Kennedy in Brookline, a
suburb of Boston, Massachusetts. Jack was their
second child and second son. Joe Kennedy Sr. was
a very successful businessman. He'd first made
money in banking and in the movies. He'd later
gone into investment banking and had successfully
made money in the stock market. By the time Jack
was born, Joe Sr. was a millionaire. His young
family lived comfortably in a big house.

Joe and Rose were Irish Roman Catholics. Their
parents and grandparents had come to the United
States from Ireland. They belonged to a Christian
religion that other Christian religions distrusted. So
even though Joe was rich, he was still an outsider
among rich people from other religions and
backgrounds. People distrusted him because he was
Catholic and Irish. This distrust was a form of
prejudice. But Joe Sr. wasn't worried. He had big
plans for himself, and he already had big plans for his
two sons. He believed they would both conquer the

forces of prejudice. Jack's older brother, Joe Jr., was big and strong. Jack admired his big brother. But he was never as good as Joe in sports and other activities.

Life in the Kennedy household was full of activity. The boys soon had younger sisters. Rosemary was born in 1918, and Kathleen came a little more than a year later. Eunice followed in 1921.

Both parents told their children many times that the United States had been good to the Kennedys. They were a well-off family, when many families were poor. Whatever benefits the family received *from* the country, Joe and Rose said, must be returned by doing some service *for* the country.

School Days

In 1926, the family moved to Riverdale, New York. Jack spent his grade-school days at Riverdale Country Day School. At thirteen, Jack went away to school for the first time. He attended Canterbury School in New Milford, Connecticut. Students boarded, or lived, at the school.

By 1930, the United States was going through a difficult economic crisis called the Great Depression. Banks and businesses failed. The stock market had crashed. Rich people suddenly became

poor. One out of four workers didn't have a job.
Poor families around the country were desperate.
Breadlines and soup kitchens—where hungry people
stood in line for handouts of food—became
common. Because of Joe Sr.'s business skills, the
Kennedy family didn't experience any of these
problems. They were still rich.

By this time, the Kennedy family had grown to
include Patricia, Bobby, Jean, and Edward, who was
called Ted or Teddy. With nine children and a
comfortable income, Rose Kennedy had servants to
do the housework. This way, she could spend more
time with her busy, noisy family. Joe Kennedy

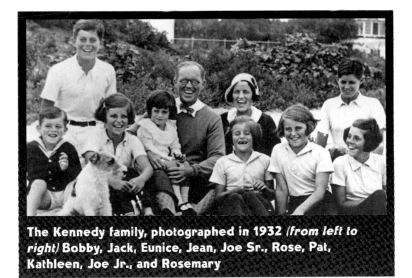

The Kennedy family, photographed in 1932 *(from left to right)* Bobby, Jack, Eunice, Jean, Joe Sr., Rose, Pat, Kathleen, Joe Jr., and Rosemary

bought other homes in West Palm Beach, Florida, and in Hyannis Port, Massachusetts.

Hyannis Port sits very close to the Atlantic Ocean. Jack came to love the sea at Hyannis Port. He learned how to handle small boats. He named his first sailboat *Victura*, which he thought meant something about winning, he said. Joe Sr. made sure his children understood about winning. He taught them to always try to be first, to be the best, even within the family. Against outsiders, family loyalty was the most important thing.

In the fall of 1931, Jack was sent to Choate Preparatory in Wallingford, Connecticut. Joe Jr. had already been there for a year. He was on the football, baseball, and hockey teams. Joe Jr. was also very good in his studies. As usual, it was going to be hard for Jack to compete with Joe.

Jack quickly formed his own circle of friends. Lemoyne (Lem) Billings and Ralph (Rip) Horton were his buddies. With several other boys, they started a club called the Muckers. The members often got into trouble. At Choate, students were not allowed to leave the school grounds without permission. But one night, after curfew, the Muckers sneaked out to the local ice-cream shop.

Jack **(right)** and his friends Lem Billings **(center)** and Rip Horton **(left)** sent this picture with a Christmas card.

On their way back to their rooms, they ran smack into the headmaster (principal)!

The boys were in danger of being expelled, and the headmaster told their parents. When Joe Kennedy arrived at the school, Jack confessed his part in the after-hours episode. He promised his father he would put more effort into his studies. All the boys were given a second chance.

A LOOK AT EUROPE

Jack was eighteen when he graduated from Choate in 1934. He had grown tall, skinny, and good looking, but he still looked much younger than his age. He often wished he were as handsome as his brother Joe. Meanwhile, his father had become involved in U.S. politics. He had strongly supported Franklin D. Roosevelt, the presidential candidate of the Democratic Party. Roosevelt had been elected. President Roosevelt was trying to help the many Americans who were suffering during the Great Depression.

As a high school graduation gift, Jack's parents had promised him a trip to London, England. His father wanted him to attend a summer session at the London School of Economics, but Jack didn't want to go. He thought the trip was supposed to be a vacation, not more school. Jack had heard about Professor Harold Laski, who ran the school. Laski was thought to be a Communist. And most people in the United States were suspicious of Communists. Communists wanted business owners, like Joe Sr., to have less power.

Joe Sr. said that he didn't expect Jack to agree with the professor's beliefs. Yet Jack's father thought it was a good idea for Jack to learn other points of view besides his own.

COMMUNISM

The Communist political system grew out of the ideas of Karl Marx. He was a German writer of the 1800s who believed that the workers would eventually take over governments and private property. Social classes would disappear, and everyone would share wealth. The Soviet Union (1922–1991) became the first Communist country. But its way of governing was somewhat different from Marx's ideas.

Under the Soviet Communist system, the government was in total control of nearly all parts of people's lives. The government owned all the tools for making money—such as factories, farms, banks, and all forms of transportation. The government paid all workers their salaries and provided all their benefits (such as health care). Owning private property was not allowed. Under this system, no one owned a business or a house. No one was extremely rich or extremely poor. The idea was for the government to run everything for the benefit of the people.

The United States runs under a different system. This is called the capitalist system. Under capitalism, the tools for making money can be owned by individuals. Owning private property is allowed. This system gives people freedom to succeed or fail in business based on their own choices.

Joe Kennedy Sr. had started out poor. But he made a lot of money under the capitalist system. Jack knew that under a Communist system, his father wouldn't have been able to succeed or make money.

Shortly after starting class, he became ill. He felt weak, and his skin turned yellow. A doctor told him he had jaundice and would have to go to the hospital. As soon as he was allowed to travel again,

Jack left London for Hyannis Port. He spent the rest of the summer trying to get well. He wasn't completely well when he started school at Princeton University in New Jersey in the fall of 1935.

Around Christmas, the jaundice came back, and Jack had to drop out of Princeton. Before the next school year began, he told his father he didn't want to return to Princeton. He wanted to go to Boston's Harvard University—where Joe Sr. and Joe Jr. had gone.

GETTING INVOLVED

The mid-1930s were exciting times at school and around the world. On college campuses, young people were taking a big interest in politics, social changes, and events in Europe. At this time, Europe seemed to be on the edge of war. The United States was pulling out of the Great Depression. Jack was becoming aware of the huge social and economic differences in the United States. As a rich man's son, Jack was teased about his rich family and easy life. But he cared about poor people and wondered what he could do to help them.

President Roosevelt was also watching events in Europe. In 1937, he named Joe Sr. to be the

U.S. ambassador to Great Britain. It was an
important position, and the appointment made
Jack's father very happy. As an Irish Catholic
outsider, he was finally breaking into U.S. politics.
Joe Jr. and Jack stayed at Harvard, but the rest of
the family moved to Britain. The British were
charmed by the handsome Kennedys, and the
Kennedys enjoyed living in London.

Ambassador Kennedy kept President Roosevelt
informed about events taking place in Britain.
Kennedy felt the United States shouldn't get
involved in a European war.

Nazi Germany, led by Adolf Hitler, was taking
over or threatening to take over various parts of
eastern Europe. Hitler had already sent Nazi troops
into Austria. In September 1938, the British prime
minister, Neville Chamberlain, met with Hitler in
Munich, Germany. Chamberlain's goal was to avoid
world war at all costs. Chamberlain agreed to let
the Germans claim part of Czechoslovakia. In
return, Hitler promised to stop seizing more land.
As a further effort to stop war, Britain and France
said they would defend Poland, another eastern
European country, if Germany attacked.

2

IS IT OUR WAR?

IN 1939, Jack was in his third year at Harvard, where he was getting his degree in political science. He had permission from Harvard to spend the spring term in Europe as part of his schoolwork. He added on his summer vacation as well.

He first visited his family in London and got to know the city and its people. But after talking with his father, Jack agreed to go on an unofficial trip. He was to observe and report back on how people in Europe were feeling about Hitler's moves.

He spent time in France and Belgium in western Europe, as well as in Poland and Latvia in eastern Europe. He went to the Soviet Union,

Turkey, and Palestine. He didn't just talk to the officials in these countries. He spent time walking the streets, talking to ordinary people.

Ambassador Kennedy continued to speak out against U.S. involvement in what he considered European politics. As a result, he became less popular with the British. They wanted the United States to help keep Hitler from taking over Europe. Joe Sr. thought Britain and France didn't stand a chance against the well-trained and well-equipped Nazi army.

Within a few months, however, Hitler had broken his promise to Chamberlain. He took control of all of Czechoslovakia. Soon afterward, he attacked Poland. Britain and France, which had pledged to defend Poland, declared war on Germany. On September 1, 1939, World War II began. Ambassador Kennedy advised Roosevelt that the United States should not become involved.

NEW PURPOSE

In the fall of 1939, Jack returned to Harvard. His time in Europe had made him much more mature and thoughtful. He began to study seriously for the first time in his life.

It was time to write his senior thesis (a long research paper). Jack had been thinking about Britain and its behavior toward Hitler before the war. After much studying, writing, and rewriting, he finished his thesis, which was called, "Appeasement at Munich." It carefully looked at the events in Europe that had led to World War II. Two of Jack's professors thought it was good enough to be published.

In June 1940, Jack graduated *cum laude* (with praise) from Harvard. His thesis earned *magna cum laude* (great praise).

After graduation, Jack Kennedy began sending his thesis to publishers. It was accepted for publication and was titled *Why England Slept*. (The title referred to the idea that England had watched and waited—instead of taking action—as events led to World War II.) His thesis became a best-seller.

Jack spent the summer of 1940 in Hyannis Port. He and his family and friends played touch football and tennis. They swam and sailed. But they also talked about whether the United States should get involved in World War II. It was the same topic people were talking about all over the country.

Only Rosemary stood outside the family circle. It had gradually become clear to the Kennedys that Rosemary was not like the rest of the family. She had wild, violent moods, and she was retreating into a world of her own. Her parents approved brain surgery, which failed miserably. Rosemary was left hardly able to speak or function without help. Finally, Joe Sr. and Rose agreed to send her to a special care center in Wisconsin.

IT'S A FACT!

Rosemary was mildly developmentally delayed. But when she was young, this situation wasn't well understood: She had a brain operation, called a lobotomy, that was supposed to help her. A lobotomy removes a part of the person's brain. Instead, the operation left her worse off. She died in January 2005, at the age of eighty-six.

THE WAR SPREADS

Meanwhile, Nazi armies had overtaken the Netherlands, Denmark, and France in western Europe. Romania in eastern Europe had fallen to the Nazis too. Only the poorly armed British army stood in the way of a German victory over all of

Europe. The United States was sending supplies and war materials to Britain. But the United States had not yet declared war. Joe Sr. still opposed U.S. involvement in the war. So his popularity continued to fall in Britain and in the United States. In October 1940, he resigned his job as ambassador and returned to the United States.

Both Jack and Joe Jr. volunteered for the U.S. armed services. In the spring of 1941, Joe was accepted as a naval air cadet. He was to learn to become a pilot. Both the U.S. Army and the U.S. Navy rejected Jack because of his history of illness. But he didn't give up. He bought gym equipment and worked out every day. Each morning, he took a cross-country run. He was determined to build up his physical health.

Jack had been around water and small boats most of his life. He felt sure that the navy could use his experience. In September 1941, he tried to join again. This time, he was accepted. But the navy gave him a job in Washington, D.C. He worked at a desk, far away from the fighting. That wasn't what Jack wanted at all. He asked to be transferred to active duty. World events worked in his favor.

The United States entered World War II after the Japanese bombed Pearl Harbor in 1941.

On December 7, 1941, the Japanese air force attacked the U.S. naval fleet at Pearl Harbor on the Hawaiian island of Oahu. The attack destroyed most of the fleet and killed many seamen. The next day, the United States joined World War II against Japan and Germany.

Six months later, the U.S. Navy sent Jack to the Naval Officers Training School at Northwestern University in Evanston, Illinois. He was given the rank of lieutenant, junior grade. Then the navy sent him to the Motor Torpedo Boat Center at Melville, Rhode Island. There he learned about patrol torpedo (PT) boats. After his training, he would become a PT skipper in Asia. He was sent to the Solomon Islands of the South Pacific Ocean.

FIRST IMPRESSIONS

One day, between classes at the Motor Torpedo Boat Center, Jack saw some people playing touch football. He joined the game. Paul Fay, the young man who was calling the plays, thought Jack was a high school kid. After all, the "kid" was dressed in an inside-out Harvard sweater, baggy trousers, and sneakers.

The "kid" turned out to be a fast and furious player, Fay said later. Much to Fay's embarrassment, the tall, thin young man turned out to be Fay's instructor in small boat handling!

CHAPTER 3

WHAT IT FEELS LIKE

THE U.S. NAVY gave command of *PT 109* to Lieutenant John F. Kennedy. This fast motorboat was about eighty feet long and was made of plywood, a very light wood. These lightweight boats were able to move quickly to escape the enemy. They could also easily get

(Above)
Lieutenant John F. Kennedy aboard *PT 109*

through the twisting waterways around the small islands in the South Pacific. PT boats had four torpedo tubes and carried four machine guns and an antiaircraft gun. But the plywood of PT boats didn't protect their crews very well from crashes or enemy fire.

In April 1943, Kennedy got his first look at *PT 109*. The boat had been through many battles and was in bad shape. He immediately ordered that the boat be cleaned and repaired.

Kennedy *(far right)* poses with his crew aboard *PT 109*.

In addition to the boat, Kennedy also inherited a few members of the PT's former crew. One was Ensign Leonard Thom, a former football star at Ohio State University. Kennedy made Ensign Thom his executive officer (second in command). Together, they chose the rest of the crew.

Most of the men thought Kennedy was too young and inexperienced to lead them. But they soon changed their minds. The PT crew liked Kennedy because he treated them fairly and worked as hard as any of them. Together, they scraped, sanded, and painted the hull, the engine room, and the lower quarters of *PT 109*. With the engine cleaned and oiled, *PT 109* was ready for duty.

First Mission

At about this time, U.S. forces were working slowly to take over Rabaul, which was under Japanese control. This port city is on the island of Papua New Guinea. On the night of August 1, 1943, word came that Japanese ships were coming toward the island. The navy sent a fleet of fifteen PT boats to meet the Japanese. It was hard to see. The crew of *PT 109* couldn't be sure if a dark shape was an enemy ship, a trick of the light, or another PT boat.

To reduce noise, *PT 109* crept along on only one engine. Lieutenant Kennedy looked into the darkness. Ensign Barney Ross was on deck standing near a machine gun. Suddenly, nineteen-year-old Harold Marney shouted, "Ship at two o'clock." This meant he'd spotted a ship to the right of *PT 109*.

A Japanese destroyer, the *Amagiri,* was almost on top of them. The crew had no time to launch a torpedo or to change course. The *Amagiri's* steel hull tore into the plywood frame of *PT 109*. Kennedy was thrown against a wall so hard he almost broke his back. His first thought was, he related afterward, so, this is how it feels to die.

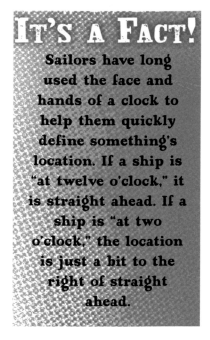

IT'S A FACT!

Sailors have long used the face and hands of a clock to help them quickly define something's location. If a ship is "at twelve o'clock," it is straight ahead. If a ship is "at two o'clock," the location is just a bit to the right of straight ahead.

The *Amagiri* had cut *PT 109* in two. The stern, or back half of the boat, was in flames. The bow section, the front, was still floating. Kennedy ordered everyone into the water. He called roll to find out who—out of his crew of twelve men—had survived the crash. Two men had been killed. Pat McMahon had been seriously burned. The other nine men, exhausted and injured, got back into the bow, which was still floating. The crew of *PT 109* had gotten through the crash, but the worst was yet to come.

SURVIVING THE CRASH

Until dawn, the survivors huddled in the bow and tried to decide what to do. In the dark, they didn't know their exact location. They knew that the Japanese occupied many of the nearby small islands. As the shadows lifted, they were in danger of being seen by the enemy.

Then what was left of *PT 109* turned over. The movement pitched them all into the water. Fortunately, Jack had figured out what supplies they had left. Besides a blinker light, they had a ship's lantern, several life jackets, a Thompson machine gun, some smaller guns, and three knives. They would have to swim to an island.

But McMahon had serious burns over half his body. He couldn't possibly make it alone. Jack cut one end of McMahon's life jacket strap.

He put the loose end of the strap in his mouth
and clamped down hard with his teeth. Slipping
under McMahon, Jack began to swim while
towing McMahon on his back. He said nothing
about his own back injury. The others tied what
supplies they had to a plank of wood. They used
the wooden plank for support in the water as
they swam.

Jack's strong, steady strokes soon took him
and McMahon out of sight of the others. Time
began to blur. Jack had no idea he had been in the
water for eight hours. Then he caught sight of an
island. He'd studied the
maps of the area before
the mission. He could tell
from the size and shape of
the land that they were
near Plum Pudding Island.
The tall trees—called
casuarina trees—would
hide them from Japanese
planes.

IT'S A FACT!
Casuarina trees are
easy to spot. They
have long needles
and thin branches.
They usually grow in
clumps along warm
seashores.

Ignoring the pain in
his back, Jack reached the rocky shore. The two
exhausted men fell under some bushes and

rested. At last, Jack sat up and looked across the water. He was overjoyed to see the plank, with nine bobbing heads alongside, nearing the shore. They too fell onto the shore and rested or slept. When the crew couldn't find any plants to eat or water to drink, Jack realized they couldn't stay there long.

After sundown, Jack swam out into Ferguson Passage. He hoped to be able to find a patrolling PT boat. He hadn't had anything to eat or drink for eighteen hours. His back was burning with pain. He wore shoes that he had saved from the wreck and carried a revolver tied around his neck. After treading water for hours, Jack was forced to admit that no patrol boats were coming. Eventually, he swam back to Plum Pudding Island.

Two days later, the entire crew swam to nearby Olasana Island. Jack again towed McMahon. On Olasana, they found coconut palm trees. They smashed coconuts on the coral rocks and drank the milk eagerly. But after three days of no food and little to drink, they got sick. Jack tried to keep the men hopeful about being rescued, but they all knew their situation was dangerous.

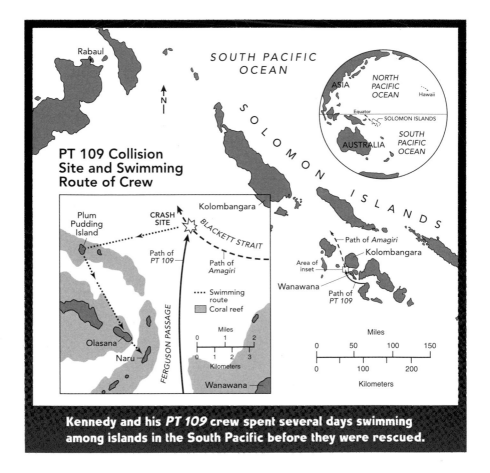

Kennedy and his *PT 109* crew spent several days swimming among islands in the South Pacific before they were rescued.

Jack and Barney Ross set off for Naru Island the next day. When they landed on a sandy shore, they found a supply of rainwater, a large wooden box of hard candy, and a canoe. The supplies had been left there by local scouts (lookouts) who were friendly to U.S. forces.

RESCUED!

The canoe that Jack and Ross had found was just big enough for one person, plus the supplies. Ross stayed on Naru while Jack started back to Olasana. When Jack arrived, a cheerful fire was burning on the shore. Two local boys had arrived in canoes and had shared some food with the happy crew.

The boys took him back to Naru in their canoe. Jack pointed to Rendova Peak. This high place could be seen from all over the area. He repeated the name "Rendova." The boys seemed to understand. Jack picked up a coconut. He scraped off some of the outer shell to make a smooth surface. Then he carved a message. It said:

NARU ISL./
NATIVE KNOWS POSIT [position]
HE CAN PILOT/11 ALIVE/
NEED SMALL BOAT
KENNEDY

Unknown to Jack, the boys were scouts. They worked for Lieutenant Reginald Evans, an Australian coast watcher. (A network of coast watchers was hidden in the Solomon Islands. They watched for enemy ships and planes and reported their positions to U.S. and Australian ships in the area.) The scouts took the coconut-shell message to Evans. Evans then sent another scout in a canoe with food, water, and a message for Kennedy.

Through Evans, a plan was set up, and a PT boat was sent to the rescue. The crew members of *PT 109* got a hero's welcome when they got to Rendova, but Jack didn't join in. He felt the loss of his two dead crew.

Jack *(right)* received a Purple Heart medal for his heroism in rescuing three of his men.

Jack refused a chance to go home and was given another boat, *PT 59*. Some of his old crew volunteered to serve with him. They kept on patrolling the waters of the Pacific Ocean. Twice they took part in rescues of other patrols.

LEAVING THE NAVY

Jack was in constant pain. The back injury from the crash had never healed well. Eventually, he became very ill with malaria. He lost twenty-five pounds. Even Jack had to admit that he was no longer fit for duty. He was forced to give up his command and was sent home to Chelsea Naval Hospital near Hyannis Port.

On weekends, Jack was allowed to leave the hospital to spend time with his family. It seemed almost like old times, except that Joe, Kathleen, and Rosemary weren't there. Joe Jr. was flying dangerous missions in Europe. He was feeling somewhat jealous of his younger brother's honors and celebrity. Against the wishes of her Catholic parents, Kathleen (Kick) had married a Protestant officer. He was also the marquess of Hartington, a member of the British upper class. Rosemary was still in a special hospital in Wisconsin.

Jack's back wasn't getting any better, and he was weak and tired. Finally, he decided to follow his doctors' advice. He had an operation on his spine in the summer of 1944. The operation didn't go well. Jack was flat on his back in a hospital bed when he received the worst blow of all. Joe Jr. had been killed in action on August 12, 1944, a little more than a year after the *PT 109* collision.

Jack fought his grief and poor health. But only a month later, Kick's husband was killed in France. She was home with the family in Hyannis Port when she got the news. They all drew closer together in their sorrow.

It's a Fact!

Joe Jr. was a bomber pilot in World War II. At the end of the war, German workers were making V-2 rockets. These rockets could take off from Germany and hit Britain. Joe Jr.'s last mission was to attack a V-2 rocket site. His plane was loaded with explosives and blew up soon after takeoff. He died instantly.

CHAPTER 4

HITTING THE CAMPAIGN TRAIL

IN NOVEMBER 1944, President Franklin Roosevelt was elected to serve a fourth term. One of Roosevelt's most important projects was to set up the United Nations (UN). This new international organization was to work for world peace. In April 1945, just two weeks before the first UN Conference was to meet, President Roosevelt died after a long illness. Vice President Harry S. Truman became president.

The first official meeting of the UN was to take place in San Francisco, California. The Hearst newspapers, a group of newspapers owned by William Randolph Hearst, offered Jack the chance to report on the conference. He was glad to accept.

Jack watched the meetings with great interest but was soon disappointed. UN members spent more time arguing among themselves than getting down to business. He realized that getting many different countries to cooperate was not easy.

Meanwhile, World War II had finally ended. The war in Europe ended first, in May 1945. The war in the Pacific took longer to finish, but it was over in September 1945. The United States came out of the war as one of the world's two superpowers. The other superpower was the Soviet Union, a wartime ally.

Serviceman's View of Conference:

Soviet Diplomacy Gets 50-50 Break

(Lt. John F. Kennedy, recently retired PT Boat hero of the South Pacific and son of Former Ambassador Joseph P. Kennedy, is covering the San Francisco United Nations Conference from a serviceman's point of view for the N. Y. Journal-American. Before the war he authored the best seller "Why England Slept.")

By JOHN F. KENNEDY
Special to the N. Y. Journal-American

SAN FRANCISCO, May 3.—The word is out more or less officially that Molotov is about to pick up his marbles and go home. He'll leave his delegation here to carry out the important detailed work. This news comes as no surprise because as the spotlight turns toward Europe and the war's ending—not only Molotov but many of the reporters are getting ready to head east.

Diplomacy might be said to be the art of who gets what and how as applied to international affairs. As Mr. Molotov gets ready to leave, Lets look at Mr. Molotov's record and see what he got and how he went about it.

His record as far as what he got was .500. He won the fight over chairmanship and the fight for the inclusion of White Russia and the Ukraine while he lost on Poland and the Argentine.

RUSSIAN DIPLOMACY.

This last fight over Argentina has been hailed as a moral victory for him but it remains to be seen how much they pay off on moral victories.

This battle, however, is worth examining as it gives good insight into Russian diplomacy at this

on the second day of the conference when a reporter asked Mr. Molotov whether he was in favor of admitting Argentina to the United Nations Conference.

He replied with what appeared sincere surprise that that was "a new question" for him and that he had no comment. Yet four days later he waged a bitter battle on the assembly floor against Argentina being admitted to the conference.

CHANGE IN ATTITUDE.

What caused this change of attitude?

The most popularly accepted theory is that he thought that by making a fight over it he could win a compromise and bring Poland in on Argentina's coat-tails.

Now no one here held any particular brief for Argentina's conduct during the war — but the South Americans did want her in. It was their belief that any Fascist tendencies that Argentina might have could be controlled better if she was joined with them than if she went her way alone.

They also felt that since she had been admitted to the conference at Chapultepec with President Roosevelt's OK, she should also be admitted here. Some of the European countries went along

Kennedy wrote this article about the first UN meeting, in San Francisco.

Atomic Bombs

In 1945, the war in Europe was winding down. But the war in the Pacific went on. Finally, President Truman decided to use the atomic bomb against Japan to make the war end sooner. The bomb was so powerful and could kill so many people at once that most people thought it would force the Japanese to surrender. But Japan kept fighting, ignoring an order to surrender. A U.S. bomber dropped the first atomic bomb on Hiroshima *(below)* on August 6, 1945. A second bomb was dropped on Nagasaki on August 9, 1945. The bombs caused terrible damage, but they did end the war. On September 2, 1945, Japan signed a formal treaty of surrender.

A FAMILY TRADITION

Jack was finished with his military service. World events were exciting, and Jack wanted to be a part of them. Both of Jack's grandfathers had been active in politics. Honey Fitz (Rose's father) had held various jobs in state and local politics. He had served as mayor of Boston, as a state legislator (lawmaker), and as a U.S. congressman. Joe Sr.'s father, Patrick Kennedy, had also been a state legislator and a state senator.

The family—especially Jack's father—had assumed that Joe Jr. would go into politics. Suddenly, Jack was the oldest Kennedy. Joe Sr.'s expectations fell on Jack's shoulders. Jack felt that he had to fill his older brother's shoes. But he still believed that he could never do things quite as well as Joe would have done them.

Jack's chance to get into politics came in 1946. U.S. congressman James Curley from the Eleventh District of Massachusetts decided to retire. The Eleventh District was a mixture of factories, worn-down apartment houses, churches, bars, and Harvard University. Jack declared his goal to run for the U.S. House of Representatives, the lower house of the U.S. Congress. He had ties with the old-time politicians through his father and grandfathers. But he also got to know the ordinary people of the Eleventh District.

Jack was friendly, but he was also shy in large groups. It wasn't easy for him to walk into a bar or factory and talk to the workers, but he did it. Sometimes he'd get so caught up in what they were saying that he'd have to be pulled away.

One of the people who opened his door to Jack was Dave Powers. Dave had just come home from serving in World War II. He was living with his widowed sister and her eight children in a low-rent apartment in the Eleventh District. Dave was surprised when a tall, young stranger held out his hand and introduced himself. He said he was running for Congress and asked Dave for his help.

Dave became one of Jack's hardest workers. He introduced Jack to people in the neighborhood. Jack wasn't a great speaker, especially in front of large groups. But people were impressed by his sincerity. Jack set up groups of young Democrats throughout the district. He had the help of men like his brother Bobby and Dave Powers, Larry O'Brien, and Lem Billings.

CONGRESSMAN AND SENATOR

On election day in 1946, Jack went to the polling place with his proud grandmother and grandfather Fitzgerald. Jack easily won his congressional election.

Jack was a representative of Massachusetts in the U.S. House of Representatives from 1946 through 1952.

Jack served the people of his district well. His office door was always open. Ted Reardon and a secretary named Mary Davis handled day-to-day business. But often a telephone caller was surprised when Congressman Kennedy himself answered. He was also informal about dressing. Sometimes he showed up for work wearing wrinkled trousers and socks that didn't match.

After three two-year terms (six years) as a congressman, Jack became frustrated with the rules in the U.S. House of Representatives. Laws were often weakened to satisfy the many needs of different groups. In 1952, he decided to run for the

U.S. Senate, the upper house of Congress. He hoped he could have more power in the Senate. His opponent was Republican senator Henry Cabot Lodge. Lodge had already served two terms in the Senate. He was fifteen years older than Jack. He was also a member of an old Protestant family in Massachusetts.

At the beginning of the 1952 campaign, Jack's back hurt so much that he was forced to use crutches. The hole in his back from the last operation had never healed. He looked thin and sickly. Jack's determination, however, was stronger than his pain. He had the will to win. This time, he made twenty-seven-year-old Bobby, who had just finished law school, his campaign manager. Except for Honey Fitz, who had died in 1950, the team that had worked so well in his congressional campaigns was together again.

Jack's sisters Eunice, Patricia, and Jean and often their mother held teas at which Jack spoke. At one tea in July, a large group of women gathered.

IT'S A FACT!

In 1916, Honey Fitz had run against Lodge's grandfather for a seat in the U.S. Senate. Honey Fitz lost.

Because of his recurring back pain, Jack campaigned for the 1952 Senate election on crutches.

After his speech, Jack moved around the room to speak to each one of the women individually, although he was on crutches at the time.

When all the votes were in on election day in November 1952, Kennedy beat Lodge. Yet in a national wave of Republican support, Dwight D. Eisenhower won the presidency on the same day. Eisenhower chose Lodge to be U.S. ambassador to the United Nations.

Around this time, Jack reached another turning point. Friends introduced him to a beautiful, educated woman named Jacqueline Bouvier. She had grown up in New York and Washington and had graduated from Vassar College (in southern New York State) and had attended the Sorbonne University in Paris, France. Her mother and stepfather lived in Newport, Rhode Island. Jacqueline's family was Catholic and, like Jack's, came from a wealthy background. She spoke French, Italian, and Spanish. Jack was very attracted to the soft-spoken, dark-haired beauty, but he didn't see her again for six months. She went to Europe, and Jack campaigned in Massachusetts.

After the election, Jack called her. They began to date frequently. Finally, Jack asked her to marry him. On September 12, 1953, they were married at

Jack met Jacqueline Bouvier in 1952. He liked her immediately.

Saint Mary's Catholic Church in Newport. He and Jacqueline moved into a redbrick house in the wealthy Georgetown area of Washington, D.C.

At this time, the United States and the Soviet Union were competing for global power. The fear of Communism gripped Americans in the 1950s. Being against Communism–the Soviet style of government–was a popular political position. While in the House of Representatives, Jack had encouraged labor leaders to talk against Communist influences within their labor unions. The goal was to stamp out these influences.

MAKING PROGRESS

During this time, Jack experienced extremely painful back problems. He had a tricky operation on his spine in October 1954 that kept him away from his job. He had also been diagnosed with Addison's disease. This illness weakens the body's ability to fight infection.

Jack had one more operation on his spine in February 1955. While he was recovering from the second surgery, Jack wrote *Profiles in Courage*. The book showed the moral courage of eight senators who had risked their careers for something they believed in. Jacqueline visited him every day and helped him with his research. *Profiles in Courage* became a best-seller. In 1957, it won the Pulitzer Prize (an annual prize given for excellence in several categories of American literature) for Biography.

In May 1955, Jack returned to his Senate office. As he walked into the Senate chamber, all the senators applauded to welcome him back. With a broad smile on his face, Jack took his seat in a back row.

Jack was beginning to make his mark in the Senate. He was well informed and able to see both sides of an issue. He

IT'S A FACT!

Joseph Pulitzer was a hugely successful U.S. newspaper publisher in the 1800s. In his will, he left a large amount of money for several awards, each of which is called the Pulitzer Prize. The categories are journalism, letters (writing), and music. In 1957, Jack was awarded five hundred dollars for a Pulitzer Prize in Biography.

weighed his decisions carefully. Jack believed strongly in the right of every person to get a good education. He felt every American should have an

equal chance to get a job and to have a decent
standard of living.

Jack's views also seemed to match an earlier
decision by the U.S. Supreme Court, the most
powerful court in the United States. In 1954, it had
made a famous civil rights decision on school
segregation (forcing black students and white
students to go to separate schools). In *Brown v.
Board of Education of Topeka,* the Court ruled that
segregation in public schools was unconstitutional
(against the U.S. Constitution). Because of the
Court's decision, states had to allow black children
and white children to go to the same schools.

THE *BROWN* CASE

The U.S. Supreme Court's desegregation decision was part of a famous
legal case. The case was called *Brown versus the Board of Education of
Topeka* (Kansas). It started when Oliver Brown, an African American,
challenged the view that his daughter couldn't go to a white school near
their home in Topeka.

The NAACP, a civil rights group, decided to use the *Brown* case to change
the laws that kept African Americans and whites from going to the same
schools. These laws said that schools could be "separate but equal." The
NAACP argued—and the U.S. Supreme Court agreed—that separate schools
would never be equal. The decision said all public schools had to be
desegregated. While desegregation got started in the mid-1950s, it was
a long time before it was completed.

Making the decision was fairly easy. Making the decision stick in all the states was harder. This was especially true in the southern states, where segregation was a way of life. Someone was going to have to take a stand and to lead the country into an era of greater civil rights.

5 ON HIS WAY

(Above) Jack speaks at the 1956 Democratic National Convention in Chicago, Illinois.

IN HIS SECOND TERM in the Senate, Jack quickly became a leader. He became a member of the powerful Senate Foreign Relations Committee. This committee pays attention to the way the United States deals with other countries. Jack was also chairperson of the Senate Subcommittee on Labor.

Jack became known as a young man in a hurry to move forward in his career. The 1956 Democratic National Convention took place in

Chicago, Illinois. Jack Kennedy was a possible
candidate for vice president. He made a speech
naming Adlai Stevenson as the Democratic Party's
presidential candidate. Stevenson would run against
President Dwight D. Eisenhower. It was Kennedy's
first nationwide television appearance. He did well,
but Senator Estes Kefauver of Tennessee became
the Democratic Party's candidate for vice president.
Jack may have been disappointed, but he went
back to his job in the Senate with even more
determination.

Jack began speaking to groups all over the
country. In the fall of 1956, he made more than
150 speeches and traveled in twenty-four states. At
first, he campaigned for Adlai Stevenson. But after
Stevenson's defeat in November, Jack continued his
speeches for his own goals. He wanted to visit
every state in the country.

GEARING UP

Even though it had taken a long time, Jack had
finally realized he was equal to his brother Joe. In
fact, Jack had many qualities that Joe had lacked.
Jack was known for his sharp wit. He had a great
ability to remember facts. Best of all, he could

laugh at himself. He cared deeply about poor
people, old people, and victims of unfairness.
Because of his passionate beliefs, he decided to try
for a more powerful job. He decided to run for
president of the United States.

On a personal level, things were also looking
up. Late in 1957, the Kennedys welcomed their first
child, Caroline. Jack and Jacqueline delighted in
their daughter. At this time, Jack started taking

Baby Caroline Kennedy was christened on December 13,
1957. She is held by Jacqueline's sister, Lee Radziwell,
while Bobby (left) and John (right) look on.

injections to reduce his back pain. A new medication helped control his Addison's disease. His health improved.

For the next few years, Jack talked to people throughout the United States. He chatted with coal miners in West Virginia and dairy farmers in Wisconsin. He listened to labor leaders in Chicago and politicians in New York. Everywhere he went, voters questioned his Roman Catholic religion. People were afraid that the pope—who lives in Rome, Italy, and is the head of the Roman Catholic Church—would run the United States if a Catholic were elected president. No Catholic had ever been president.

At one meeting, the matter came into the open. A student stood up and asked, "Senator Kennedy, can a Catholic become president?" Jack said that he had taken an oath of loyalty to his country when he had entered the navy. He'd taken a similar oath when he became a congressman and when he became a senator. "If I was qualified to serve my country in those other capacities, I am qualified to serve it as president." He added, "No one asked my brother Joe if he had divided loyalties when he

volunteered and died for his country." The
audience applauded his answer.

By 1959, Jack's campaign was running
in high gear. Jack bought a plane so he could
travel quickly. His campaign staff was working
smoothly. His manager was Bobby. Ted Sorensen,
Larry O'Brien, Ken O'Donnell, Dave Powers,
Steve Smith, and Pierre Salinger also played
important roles. The presidential primaries
were next.

BISHOPS' APPROVAL

The fifty-member Council of Methodist Bishops met in Washington in
April 1959 and invited Jack to attend. He was quizzed on his religion
and its possible effect on his ability to hold office.

"I am a strong Catholic," Jack replied. "I come from a strong Catholic
family. But I regret the fact that some people get the idea that the
Catholic Church favors a church-state tie. I will make my decisions
according to my own judgment of the best interests of all people. I
do not intend to disavow [give up] either my religion or my beliefs in
order to win the presidency. If the outcome of this campaign was
settled on the day I was born, then the whole nation is the loser."

The bishops applauded his talk. They admitted that they admired his
honesty, courage, and his balanced stand. It was quite a victory and
another turning point for Jack.

THE PRESIDENTIAL PRIMARIES

Each of the major political parties–the Democrats and the Republicans–hold presidential primary elections in many but not all states. These early elections don't actually elect anyone to be president. Two or more candidates of the same political party compete for votes. Primaries show how popular the various candidates within the same party are. In many states, winning a primary election means winning the party's delegates in that state. These delegates go to the party's national convention and choose the party's candidate to run for president.

IT'S A FACT!

Only one Catholic had ever before run for U.S. president—Al Smith of New York. In 1928, he lost by a huge number of votes.

The 1960 presidential primary elections began early in March in New Hampshire. Kennedy won there with a high number of votes. But Democratic senator Hubert Humphrey of Minnesota also wanted to be president. He entered the Wisconsin primary. Soon after winning in New Hampshire, Jack decided to challenge Humphrey in Wisconsin.

Bobby advised Jack not to take this step. Humphrey was very well known in Wisconsin. Wisconsin and Minnesota are neighboring states. They are also alike in many ways. For example, both are dairy and farming states. No one could mistake Jack Kennedy as a farm boy. Most of the people in Wisconsin followed the Protestant faith. Jack's Catholic faith would be a big obstacle. Jack went ahead with his plan anyway.

In bitter, wintry weather, he walked the streets of small towns in Wisconsin. At first, people seemed to disappear when they saw him. Everyone knew that Kennedy was a rich man's son. He flew in on his own plane. Humphrey arrived on a bus. Gradually, the picture changed. Crowds kept

IT'S A FACT!
Kennedy named his plane, *Caroline*, after his two-year-old daughter.

getting larger. People began to realize that this rich man's son cared about them. He had studied the problems faced by farmers, small dairy owners, and people in small businesses. He seemed to care

Hubert Humphrey *(right)* was another Democrat who wanted to run for president in 1960.

about people without jobs. He wanted decent wages for people with jobs. On primary day, April 5, 1960, Wisconsin Democrats chose Kennedy as their presidential candidate.

Kennedy and Humphrey were opponents again in the West Virginia primary. The state faced huge problems of rising poverty, too few jobs, and too little health care. Kennedy had to answer questions about his religion again and again. On May 10, West Virginians went to the polls. They gave Kennedy 212,000 votes to 136,000 for Humphrey. Humphrey took himself out of the presidential race.

THE NATIONAL CONVENTIONS

Several weeks before the Democratic National Convention, the Republican Party held its own national convention. Republican delegates chose Vice President Richard Nixon as their 1960 presidential candidate. Nixon and Jack had been congressmen together.

The 1960 Democratic National Convention took place in the Los Angeles Sports Arena in Los Angeles, California. On July 11, voting for the candidates began. Some delegates were supporting Senator Lyndon Johnson of Texas. Most were for Kennedy. The final vote for Jack was 806 (out of 1500), and eventually the convention voted to change all its votes for Kennedy.

The convention wasn't over yet. A vice-presidential candidate had to be chosen. Texas senator Lyndon Johnson had won 409 presidential votes. Jack felt sure that Johnson would be the strongest vice-presidential running mate. Texas had

Lyndon Johnson (right) agreed to be Jack's vice-presidential running mate.

a large number of voters. And Jack also hoped that choosing Johnson might influence some southern and western states to vote for him. The next day, all the convention delegates and party leaders were on hand to unite behind their new leader. Jack chose Lyndon Johnson to be his vice president. The delegates ratified, or confirmed, his choice.

CHAPTER 6

"ASK WHAT YOU CAN DO"

(Above) Jack gave many speeches to large crowds during his presidential campaign in 1960.

RUNNING FOR PRESIDENT was a hard job. Jack worked eighteen-hour days. He made brief personal appearances in many small communities and wrote speeches while traveling on the airplane *Caroline*. In ten weeks, Jack traveled 78,654 miles. Everywhere he went, the crowds got bigger.

Toward the end of the campaign, four debates between Kennedy and Nixon took place on TV. These were the first televised political debates ever to be held in the United States. They gave the American public a chance to see and compare both candidates. At the first debate, held in Chicago, Nixon looked stiff and ill at ease. Nixon presented his ideas well, but he didn't answer Jack's arguments in a strong way. Jack looked at ease, and he was funny. His sincerity impressed TV audiences. The debates marked a turning point in the campaign.

In 1960, presidential candidates debated on national television for the first time in U.S. history. This family is watching one of the debates.

Jack's last appearance was at a huge rally in Boston on the night before the election. The next morning, November 8, 1960, was election day. Election results were slowly coming in. For the first time, computers were being used on a large scale to count votes. At 7:15 P.M., newspeople told viewers they believed Richard Nixon would win big. An hour later, they said it would be a Kennedy victory.

ELECTION NIGHT

Jack finally began to gain in electoral votes. (The candidate who gets the most votes within a state wins all of that state's electoral votes. The number of electoral votes a state has is based on its population.) At 3:00 A.M., word came that Nixon would make an appearance at the Ambassador Hotel in Los Angeles. Nixon said, "If the present trend continues, . . . Senator Kennedy will be the next president of the United States." But this wasn't the same as saying Nixon was giving up.

At 4:00 A.M., everyone went to bed. In the morning, no definite change had happened. The only one who was sure of the outcome was young Caroline. When she first saw her father that morning, she said, "Good morning, Mr. President."

Jack laughed and then took his daughter down to the beach.

Although the day was cold and windy, almost all of the Kennedys were out that morning walking along the bleak shore of the Atlantic Ocean. Officers from the Secret Service appeared about 7:30 A.M. Jack took that as a good sign. The Secret Service was always assigned to guard the president. Jack had won!

The president-elect and his wife returned to Georgetown. In late November, Jacqueline gave birth to a baby boy. They called him John Fitzgerald Kennedy Jr. As soon as John Jr. was strong enough to travel, Jack, Jacqueline, Caroline, and her baby brother went to Palm Beach, Florida, for the Christmas holidays.

NAMING A CABINET

Meanwhile, Jack started forming his staff and cabinet (group of advisers). He asked Sargent Shriver (Eunice's husband), Larry O'Brien, and Bobby to pull together the best possible choices for important posts in the new administration. He also consulted some of his former Harvard professors. He wanted to appoint the very best people he could.

Jack and his family returned to Georgetown in January. The presidential inauguration–when he would be sworn in as president–would take place on January 20, 1961. Reporters parked themselves outside the front door of the Kennedys' redbrick house.

Some presidents made their choices of staff to repay people within the party who'd helped them get elected. Jack chose people based on how smart they were and what kind of character they had. Party loyalty wasn't the main consideration. For example, he asked Robert McNamara, a Republican, to be secretary of defense. He named Douglas Dillon, another Republican, to be secretary of the treasury.

Jack had one appointment he was slow to tell reporters about. He wanted Bobby to be attorney general, the highest law officer of the United States. But Bobby wasn't at all sure it was a good idea. Bobby protested about what he thought the press would say. He thought reporters would see Jack's move as just a way of keeping things in the family.

Both brothers met the press, and Jack told the reporters his decision. The reporters quickly asked just the kind of questions Bobby had feared. Jack explained that he trusted Bobby more than anyone

Jack appointed his
brother Robert (right)
to be attorney general.

else he could think of. He trusted his judgment,
his ability, and his commitment.

THE INAUGURATION

On January 19, the night before inauguration day,
it snowed heavily. Cars were stranded in snow
drifts. Many people walked in snow over their
ankles. These hardships made the coming
inauguration all the more exciting. In the morning,
Jack went to Mass at nearby Trinity Church. After
Mass, Jack and Jacqueline went to the White House

to have coffee with the Eisenhowers. Cheering
crowds lined the still snowy streets.

The old and new presidential parties arrived at
the steps of the U.S. Capitol (where Congress
meets) around 12:30 P.M.
The president's swearing-in
ceremony would take
place there. Jack put his
right hand on the family
Bible. He spoke the words
that pledged him to
uphold the Constitution
and the laws of the United
States to the best of his
ability. He charged his
listeners, both in
Washington and around
the nation, to "ask not
what your country can do
for you; ask what you can do for your country."
Millions of people realized they had elected a
president with a fresh spirit who was interested in
new ideas.

IT'S A FACT!
The president-elect
had asked all the
men to wear formal
clothes. This clothing
was part of an old
tradition. The
clothing included a
high hat, called a top
hat. Kennedy carried
his top hat but only
once in a while
remembered to put
it on.

CHAPTER 7

GETTING TO WORK

WHEN THE EXCITEMENT of inauguration
day ended, Jack lost no time in getting down to
business. He called his first meeting the very next
day, on January 21, 1961. In his office, Jack awaited
the arrival of his team. Soon presidential aide Ted
Sorensen and special assistant Arthur Schlesinger Jr.
came in. They were followed by Pierre Salinger,
Jack's press secretary—the person who'd be talking
with the press. Kenny O'Donnell, the person to
contact for a meeting with the president, showed
up. So did Larry O'Brien, Jack's contact with
Congress. Dave Powers, Jack's personal aide, was
also on hand.

NEW IDEAS

One of President Kennedy's favorite new ideas was the Peace Corps. Its goal was to encourage world peace and friendship. Peace Corps volunteers would be skilled people from the United States. Their job was to help people in poor countries help themselves.

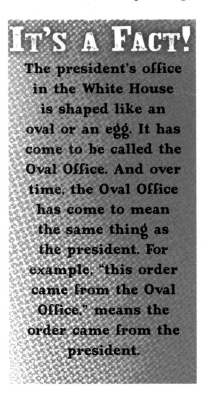

IT'S A FACT!

The president's office in the White House is shaped like an oval or an egg. It has come to be called the Oval Office. And over time, the Oval Office has come to mean the same thing as the president. For example, "this order came from the Oval Office," means the order came from the president.

Jack set up the Peace Corps by executive order. (These are like laws, but they don't have to be approved by Congress.) The first volunteers started their training in the spring of 1961. They were mostly young people who wanted to share their skills and energy with the people of poor nations. Peace Corps volunteers taught school, built roads, bridges, schools, and health centers, and shared farming skills.

The Peace Corps gave people in South America, Central America, Africa, and Asia a new

Jack greets a group of Peace Corps volunteers.

idea of the United States. Volunteers lived and worked with the people they'd come to help. They learned and spoke their languages. They went only to countries where they were invited. Peace Corps volunteers really cared about helping people, and they liked what they were doing. The Peace Corps began with five hundred volunteers. A year and a half later, nearly five thousand Peace Corps volunteers were working in forty-five countries around the world.

FIGHTING FOR CIVIL RIGHTS

Not all of President Kennedy's ideas met with such success. Laws to guarantee civil rights were mostly a failure. Many African Americans, especially in the southern United States, were treated unjustly. They couldn't eat at whites-only restaurants or go to whites-only theaters. Desegregation was slow. In some areas, African American children still weren't going to the same schools as white children. African Americans had a harder time going to college or getting good jobs.

These problems were part of a larger problem of racial discrimination. As a congressman and senator, Jack had voted for every civil rights bill that had been introduced. But as president, he saw that a group of southern Democrats and conservative Republicans were blocking every civil rights bill that went to Congress.

At first, Jack got around this problem by carrying out his civil rights plan by executive order. He wanted not only to get rid of racial discrimination but he also wanted to teach people that discrimination was wrong.

Bobby and Jack worked closely together during the civil rights struggle. For example, Bobby and

Bobby worked closely with Jack on civil rights. Here he speaks in front of a Senate committee in favor of some of Jack's civil rights proposals.

his team had quiet meetings with school boards in southern cities, such as Atlanta, Georgia; Dallas, Texas; Memphis, Tennessee; and New Orleans, Louisiana. As a result, with little fuss, many schools were integrated. This meant African Americans and whites could go to the same schools. African Americans and whites used the same facilities in railroad stations, bus stations, and airlines.

Yet the president had little success getting Congress to pass the civil rights laws he wanted. So he used lawsuits, executive orders, and personal actions as powerful tools in the cause of civil rights. Jack publicly supported the idea of equal rights. He was able to force many small changes that gave people a new way to think about civil rights.

THE CIVIL RIGHTS MOVEMENT

The civil rights movement was in full swing when Jack took office. The movement's leader was Martin Luther King Jr. African Americans—joined by many northern whites—were protesting against segregated public facilities (restaurants, stores, bus stations, and schools). Their protests didn't involve violence of any kind.

In 1961, Freedom Riders rode buses to different southern towns and cities to help integrate public facilities. Freedom Riders were mostly young people, both black and white, from many parts of the United States. White southerners who wanted to keep facilities segregated often attacked Freedom Riders, while southern police officers watched. Jack—and Bobby as attorney general—often sent U.S. troops to protect King and his peaceful protesters from angry white mobs.

Many people did not agree with the views of the Freedom Riders. Angry protesters set fire to this Freedom Riders bus in 1961.

Jack committed himself and the country "to
the proposition that race has no place in American
life or law." He talked about laws he would send
to Congress. But he also said that "Legislation
[laws] cannot solve the problem alone. It must be
solved in the homes of every American." He
pointed out the basic injustice of racial
discrimination. "We are confronted primarily with
a moral issue. . . . Now the time has come for this
nation to fulfill its promise. . . . Those who do
nothing are inviting shame as well as violence.
Those who act boldly are recognizing right as well
as reality." He later sent to Congress the broadest
civil rights bill that had ever been suggested.

CHAPTER 8

FOREIGN POLICY

(Above) In 1961, Jack answers questions from the press about U.S. involvement in Cuba.

EVEN AS A YOUNG MAN, Jack had had a strong interest in how the United States shaped its relationships with other countries. Foreign policy came into the spotlight early in his presidency—but not in a positive way.

THE BAY OF PIGS

One of Jack's worst foreign policy failures
happened shortly after he took office. The large
island of Cuba sits just ninety miles south of
Florida. A few years before, Fidel Castro and a
band of rebels had overthrown the government
of the Cuban dictator Fulgencio Batista. The U.S.
government had supported Batista. Under
Castro's leadership, Cuba had become a
Communist country. The U.S. government was
worried about having a Communist neighbor.
Some U.S. government officials decided to set up
an attack on Castro's forces. The plan organizers
would hire fourteen hundred Cuban exiles
(people who had left Cuba). This group was
called Cuban Brigade 2506.

The U.S. Central Intelligence Agency (CIA)
had formed the plan before Jack took office. (This
agency secretly gathers information about foreign
groups.) The CIA wanted the Cuban Brigade to
take care of the entire operation. The CIA thought
that once Brigade 2506 had landed in Cuba, the
Cuban people would revolt against Castro. The Bay
of Pigs, along the coast in western Cuba, was to be
the landing place.

When Jack first heard about the plan, he was shocked. But his military staff advised him to go ahead with it. Jack had his doubts. Other members of his staff also felt unsure, but they didn't speak out very forcefully. Jack reluctantly gave his consent.

The invasion began on Sunday, April 17, 1961. The planners hadn't become familiar with conditions at the Bay of Pigs. They also didn't have good information about Castro's military strength. Castro's small air force sank two ships that were carrying weapons, communication equipment, food, and medical supplies. The Cuban air force shot down half of the U.S. planes sent to protect the mission. As a result, supplies never reached the Cuban exiles on the beach.

The Cuban underground—a secret group in Cuba that was supposed to encourage the Cuban people to support the invaders—never knew about the plan. Without supplies, weapons, or air protection, Cuban Brigade 2506 was doomed. Its members fought on bravely until they were killed or captured.

The doomed venture ended on April 20, 1961. Although the plan had been set up before Jack took office, he refused to avoid his responsiblity. "As chief executive, it was my responsibility," he said. He did learn a lesson, though. From then on, he made sure he looked at all sides of a question. And he never again made a decision quickly.

MEETINGS IN EUROPE

Another problem for Jack was how to deal with the Soviet Union, the world's most powerful Communist nation. Its leader, Premier Nikita Khrushchev, invited Kennedy to meet with him in Vienna, Austria. Kennedy agreed. He wanted to

Jack met with Soviet leader Nikita Khrushchev (left) to open communications with the Soviet Union.

THE SPACE RACE

Some of Jack's goals were in answer to strides made by the Soviets. For example, the Soviet Union had launched a space capsule and had sent a man into space to orbit Earth. Jack was eager to do even more. His goal was to land a person on the moon by the end of the twentieth century. (This event took place in 1969.)

But small steps had to come first. Alan Shepard became the first American to make a spaceflight. John Glenn became the first American to orbit Earth. Between October 4, 1961, and October 3, 1962, the United States placed forty-six satellites in orbit. The country launched four space probes to gather information about weather, communications, and navigation.

During this period, the Soviet Union and the United States were competing with each other. Each country's leadership in science, engineering, and national defense was measured, in part, by its success in space.

John Glenn, the first American to orbit Earth

meet Khrushchev so that they might understand each other better. Jacqueline went with her husband to Europe.

Before going to Austria, Jack and Jacqueline visited President Charles de Gaulle of France. France wanted to develop its own atomic bomb. Jack hoped to help President de Gaulle see that the fewer nations who had the bomb, the safer all nations would be. This wasn't so successful. But with her French background and classy style, Jacqueline was a hit with the French. The Kennedys also stopped in Britain, where Jack met with British prime minister Harold Macmillan.

The Kennedys went on to Austria and Jack's meeting with Khrushchev. Both leaders headed great nations. But they each had very different

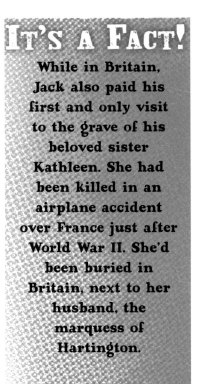

IT'S A FACT!
While in Britain, Jack also paid his first and only visit to the grave of his beloved sister Kathleen. She had been killed in an airplane accident over France just after World War II. She'd been buried in Britain, next to her husband, the marquess of Hartington.

political systems. The two countries had two points of disagreement. One disagreement was about a treaty to stop testing nuclear weapons. The Soviet Union would not agree to let people inspect (look at) its nuclear test sites. Without inspection, the United States would have no way of knowing whether the Soviet Union was obeying the rules of the treaty. While the two leaders didn't reach agreement, they did promise to keep in touch with each other.

The other disagreement involved the U.S., British, and French troops that were still in Berlin, Germany. After World War II, the Allies–Britain, France, the Soviet Union, and the United States–had divided Germany into sections. Each ally controlled one section. The Soviets set up their section under a Communist government and called it East Germany. The other allies combined their sections and allowed a democratic government to form. This section was called West Germany. The overall capital city of Berlin, however, was located in the Soviet zone. But because the city was so important, it was divided into two parts. The Soviets controlled East Berlin. Troops from Britain, France, and the United States were still in West Berlin.

Khrushchev wanted only Soviet troops in both parts of Berlin. But Jack knew that if this happened, about 2 million West Berliners would fall under Communist control. He refused to let that happen. Meanwhile, about 3.5 million East Germans had fled their homes to gain their freedom in West Berlin. In response, Khrushchev ordered the building of the Berlin Wall. This concrete and barbed-wire barrier cut through central Berlin, separating East Germans from West Germans. Building the wall shocked the democratic world. It wouldn't be the last time Khrushchev shocked Kennedy.

THE CUBAN MISSILE CRISIS

In 1962, Kennedy learned that for months, Soviet ships had been delivering equipment to Cuba. When asked about this, the Soviet government had said that the shipments had only defensive weapons in case the United States attacked Cuba. On the outside, Jack was calm and cool. In private, he was furious with Khrushchev for lying to him. Jack quickly set up a meeting of top officials, trusted friends, and military advisers. The group became known as the Executive Committee, or ExCom.

ExCom's members were sharply divided about what should be done. Some wanted to immediately bomb the missile sites and to invade Cuba. Jack and Bobby felt that this action would bring on an all-out nuclear war. Others thought that a naval blockade might stop the building of the missile base. (A naval blockade would stop more Soviet ships from being able to bring equipment to Cuba.) Bobby and McNamara favored this idea, and that was the course of action Jack decided to follow.

On Monday, October 22, 1962, President Kennedy spoke to the American people on television. He told them exactly what was happening. The whole nation was worried. The week dragged on. Messages flew back and forth between Khrushchev and Kennedy. No breakthrough happened. Then the Soviets sent eighteen cargo ships toward Cuba. Soviet submarines were on hand to protect the cargo ships.

The president sent a message to Khrushchev. Jack demanded that the ships and submarines turn back. He further demanded that the Soviets take apart the missile bases and take away the missiles from Cuba. Jack warned Khrushchev that the U.S. Navy was going to stop the Soviet ships if they kept on their course. Once the ships were stopped, the navy would take away any equipment on board.

The cargo ships and their submarines drew closer. Finally, they stopped to await further orders. At the end of the week, Khrushchev ordered the Soviet ships to turn around and head back to the Soviet Union.

On Friday evening, October 26, 1962, the president got a message from Khrushchev that hinted at an agreement. The message was vague. Yet it seemed to be saying that the Soviet Union would take away the missiles if the United States would promise not to invade Cuba. But on Saturday, Khrushchev sent another message that was the opposite of Friday's message.

IT'S A FACT!
To mark the tense time, the Kennedys gave each member of ExCom an expensive silver calendar made by Tiffany, a well-known jewelry company in New York City. The calendar marked the critical thirteen days of the Cuban Missile Crisis. The calendar also included the initials of both the president and the ExCom member.

LIFE AT THE WHITE HOUSE

Under the Kennedys, a big change in lifestyle took place at the White House. Jack and Jacqueline were gracious hosts at dinners where people talked about culture and politics. The couple set the pace for lively discussions.

Jacqueline, by herself, set a new standard for how a First Lady should look and act. Elegant and educated, she was both fashionable and intelligent. Famous dressmakers created her gowns, which dazzled the public. Jacqueline wanted to remake the White House to look like it did in the past. She asked the people of the United States to help her find antiques that might once have been part of the White House's furnishings. People from all over the land came up with ideas and furniture.

Jack and Jacqueline hosted fancy parties at the White House.

Even though he was a busy president, Jack still found time to romp with his children. One of John Jr.'s favorite games was one he made up himself. He hid behind the movable panel in his father's desk. Jack had to rap on the panel and ask if the bunny was home. John Jr. then jumped out, a delighted smile on his face, while his father acted surprised. Sometimes Caroline, dressed in her mother's high heels, popped in on a meeting. Life at the Kennedy White House was never dull.

Jack decided to answer only the first message. He said the United States would accept the Soviet offer to remove the missiles from Cuba under the eye of the United Nations. In return, the United States promised to stop the naval blockade and not to invade Cuba. In secret, Jack also agreed to remove U.S. missiles from Turkey. (This nation shared a border with the Soviet Union at the time.) The ExCom waited tensely for Khrushchev's reply.

Finally, Khrushchev answered. "The Soviet government has ordered the dismantling of bases and dispatching of equipment from the USSR . . . I appreciate your assurance that the United States will not invade Cuba." Nuclear war had been avoided. And people around the world sighed with relief.

CHAPTER

9 REACHING FOR PEACE

THE WORLD WAS a tense place in the early 1960s. The United States and the Soviet Union continued to compete on every level. Both countries had powerful weapons. Nothing was stopping them.

VISITS TO BERLIN AND IRELAND

President Kennedy visited West Germany in June 1963. The Soviets had built the Berlin Wall after his 1961 visit to Europe. It was still there, keeping apart German families, friends, and neighbors. Jack spoke to a huge crowd in the city square of West Berlin. Jack told them:

There are many people in the world today
who really don't understand, or say they don't,
what is the great issue between the free world
and the Communist world. Let them come to
Berlin! . . . All free men, wherever they may
live, are citizens of Berlin, and therefore, as a
free man, I take pride in the words, "Ich bin
ein Berliner [I am a Berliner]!

From Berlin, Kennedy went to Ireland, the
home of his ancestors. The people treated him like
a long lost son. Jack's great-grandfather, Patrick
Kennedy, had been born in Dunganstown in
County Wexford. Jack's cousin, Mrs. Mary Ryan,
laid out a fine party in her yard. Every relative for
miles around was an honored guest. After the party,
Jack left for New Ross, Ireland.

Jack's great-grandfather had left New Ross to
go to the United States. The people in New Ross
presented Jack with a beautiful gold box. Symbols
of the two Irish clans—the Kennedys and the
Fitzgeralds—were on the box. Jack was deeply
touched and thanked them.

Jack's enjoyment and his quick Irish wit won
their affection. Jack looked around at his relatives.

Jack poses with his cousins during his trip to Ireland in 1963.

"I'm glad to see," he remarked, "a few of the cousins didn't catch the boat." Jack returned to the United States with the trust of the German people and the hearts of the Irish.

THE MARCH ON WASHINGTON

Meanwhile, the civil rights movement was making progress. On August 28, 1963, the historic March on Washington took place. About 250,000 people—from all ethnic groups from all over the country—marched from the Washington Monument to the Lincoln Memorial in Washington, D.C. The march was the largest public gathering that had ever been held in the capital city.

The huge crowd was quiet and orderly. Many people listened with tears in their eyes as they heard Martin Luther King's ringing words: "I have a dream that my four little children will one day live in a nation where they will be judged not by the color of their skin, but by the content of their character. . . . I have a dream," he said again and again. He talked about the day when peace and equality would simply be the way things were.

IT'S A FACT!

In August 1963, Jacqueline gave birth early to another baby boy. The parents named him Patrick. From the very beginning, the baby had a hard time breathing. He died when he was only two days old. Both Jack and Jacqueline had been looking forward to adding to their family. They had promised Caroline and John a baby brother. The entire family grieved over Patrick's death.

After the march, the president invited several important African American civil rights leaders to the White House. Jack led them to his private quarters. When he learned that most of them hadn't had a chance to eat all day, he had food brought in. They discussed ways to bring about the civil rights changes that were so badly needed. When the leaders left, they felt that Jack Kennedy was a strong fighter on their side.

CRAFTING A TREATY

Jack had not given up his goal to get the United States and the Soviet Union to make a treaty that stopped nuclear testing. He had laid the groundwork for the treaty earlier in 1963, when he had met with Khrushchev in Europe. Jack made a huge effort to reach this goal. Talks with the Soviets took place. Jack's efforts began to show success. Britain, the Soviet Union, and the United States had agreed on the main points of a treaty that banned nuclear tests above the ground. (They could still test underground.) Officials from the three nations put their initials on the treaty in Moscow, the Soviet capital city. But, to be fully signed, it needed the Senate's approval. Jack went on television and told the American people, "This treaty is . . . an important first step—a step toward peace, a step toward reason, a step away from war."

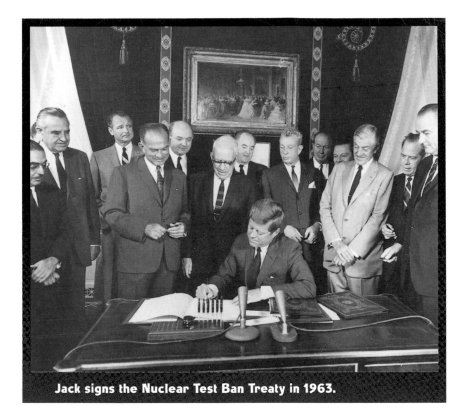

Jack signs the Nuclear Test Ban Treaty in 1963.

On September 24, 1963, the U.S. Senate approved, or ratified, the Nuclear Test Ban Treaty. As he signed the treaty, Jack said, "The age of nuclear energy has been full of fear, yet never empty of hope. Today the fear is a little less and the hope is a little greater. . . . I hereby pledge, on behalf of the United States, if this treaty fails it will not be our doing."

THE WAR IN VIETNAM

Signing the Nuclear Test Ban Treaty may have been Jack's most important success as president. But he still had many serious problems. One of the most serious was what to do about the conflict in Vietnam (1957–1975), a war-torn country in Southeast Asia. North Vietnam and South Vietnam had been divided for many years. Each part of the country wanted to rule the other. This conflict led to civil war. North Vietnam got its main support from Communist China. The United States was backing South Vietnam.

By the early 1960s, the United States had agreed to send military advisers and supplies to South Vietnam. Over time, Jack became uncomfortable with that decision. Yet the United States kept sending more advisers and more supplies every year. And every year, North Vietnam showed no signs of giving up. At the same time, the war itself was creating a serious division among people in the United States. Many viewed the conflict as a civil war that had to be decided by the Vietnamese people themselves— without the help of Communist China or the United States.

THE VIETNAM STORY

France had been in control of Vietnam since the mid-1800s. Between 1946 and 1954, Vietnamese rebel groups fought France to gain self-rule. These groups defeated France in 1954. In that year, an international meeting divided Vietnam into North Vietnam and South Vietnam. The meeting also called for an election in 1956 to unite Vietnam under one government.

North Vietnam was under Communist control. Its leader was Ho Chi Minh. He had strong ties with Communist China. Ngo Dinh Diem had been chosen as the leader of South Vietnam. He had U.S. backing. But Diem's government was harsh and wasn't interested in helping the Vietnamese people. He refused to allow the 1956 election to take place. His decisions caused a civil war to break out.

One group of Vietnamese people supported President Diem. Another group, called the Viet Cong, supported Ho Chi Minh. The Viet Cong were trained in guerrilla warfare and were aided by Communist China. (Guerrilla warfare involves striking quickly and secretly and then disappearing into the countryside.)

Ho Chi Minh

While Eisenhower (the president before Kennedy) was still president, South Vietnam had asked the United States for help in fighting the Viet Cong's guerrilla raids. Diem's army—which had only been trained in traditional warfare—was having no success against the Viet Cong. President Eisenhower sent supplies and military advisers to help train the South Vietnamese army in guerrilla warfare. Jack was left with this commitment when he became president. Late in 1961, he sent more advisers, helicopters, and supplies.

Jack had slowly come to share this point of view. He had come to believe that the war in Vietnam was a political struggle within that country. He didn't see a reason for the U.S. military to be there. He ordered the U.S. Department of Defense to draw up a plan to end all U.S. involvement in Vietnam.

Meanwhile, Jack started looking toward the 1964 presidential election. As it drew nearer, Jack needed Vice President Johnson's help in Johnson's home state of Texas. The Democrats in Texas were bitterly divided into two camps. Some supported his civil rights views. Others did not. Jack wanted to be re-elected. To win he would have to be careful about how much he talked about civil rights.

10

A TRAGIC ENDING

JACK KENNEDY knew that some people in Texas, a southern state, didn't approve of his stand on civil rights. But Jack was sure that differences of opinion could be solved through reason and goodwill.

On the morning of November 22, Jack met in the hotel parking lot in Fort Worth with

(Above) Jack at his desk in the Oval Office

local workers, such as mechanics, truck drivers, secretaries, clerks, and housewives. Before leaving for lunch with the Fort Worth Chamber of Commerce, Jacqueline appeared in the hotel dining room. She looked stunning in a fashionable pink suit and a matching hat. People sighed in admiration. Reporters gathered around her. The president was delighted by the attention to his wife. He joked, "Why is it no one cares what Lyndon and I wear?"

A short plane hop took them from Fort Worth to Dallas. When their plane landed at Love Field, the president and Jacqueline received huge cheers. People kept pushing their hands through the airport fence to try to touch the president. The mayor's wife presented Jacqueline with a bouquet of red roses.

The Secret Service had become concerned about the president's safety. It had shipped a bubble-top car to Dallas for the president's use. The top was a removable, see-through cover. Spectators and occupants could see, while, at the same time, it protected the riders from weather or the threats of the crowds. But the weather was warm and sunny. So far, the welcome had been warm and sincere. Fears for the president's safety faded away. Jack insisted that the bubble top be removed.

Jack and Jacqueline received a warm welcome in Dallas.

THE DALLAS MOTORCADE

About 250,000 people lined the streets in Dallas along the route of the presidential motorcade. The cars approached Dealey Plaza, a wide, grass-covered area. Nearby was the Texas School Book Depository, a dullorange brick building. A Secret Service agent drove the car. Another agent sat

Jack and Jacqueline ride through the streets of Dallas.

next to him with a rifle close at hand. Governor John Connally and his wife, Nellie, sat in front. Jacqueline and the president were in the back seat. Secret Service agents also rode in a car following the presidential party.

Nellie Connally turned around and said to the president, "You can't say Dallas wasn't friendly." At that moment, a sharp, cracking sound pierced the air. Jacqueline, who had been waving to the people on her left, turned to face Jack. Jack's hand went to his throat, and he began to fall forward. At almost the same time, Governor Connally gave a sharp cry and bent over. Both President Kennedy and John Connally had been shot. Seconds later, another shot hit the president in the head.

Jacqueline saw Clint Hill, a Secret Service man, trying to climb from the street onto the back of the car. She crawled toward Hill and held out her hand to him. He scrambled in and pushed Jacqueline down. He threw himself over the president's body to shield him.

The president's car raced to the nearest hospital, Parkland Memorial. Agents radioed ahead. Doctors met the car at the hospital entrance. They rushed Jack into Trauma Room One. Governor Connally was taken to another emergency room. The doctors did everything they could to save the president, but it was impossible. Jack had no pulse and no blood pressure. John Connally's wound was serious, but he would survive.

Vice President Johnson didn't know if the shooting was part of a group effort or the act of one person. He decided he should get back to Washington at once. In a short time, the president's body was carried onto Air Force One, the president's plane. Jacqueline, Vice President Johnson, his wife, Lady Bird, and other members of the presidential party got on board.

Inside the plane, Judge Sarah Hughes of Texas gave Lyndon Johnson the presidential oath of office. Lyndon Johnson became the thirty-sixth president of the United States. Dazed with shock, Jacqueline Kennedy stood by the new president. She seemed not to notice her bloodstained clothes. They carried the blood Jack had shed in the car.

IT'S A FACT!

The president's plane is called Air Force One. In 1961, the Kennedys changed the colors of Air Force One from orange to blue, silver, and white. They had a designer remake the inside of the plane to be more comfortable. Jacqueline brought in fine furniture and decorated the walls with fine paintings.

A FINAL FAREWELL

On November 23, President Kennedy's body lay in a flag-draped casket within the Capitol Building. All day and all evening, people filed past the casket. Lines of people stood in bitter cold for hours, waiting for a chance to say good-bye to the young, inspirational president.

After the last mourner left, the doors of the Capitol Building were closed to the public. Jacqueline and Caroline slipped into the building for one last visit. They knelt before the closed casket and said some prayers. Caroline reached up and touched the flag draping the casket, as though the act could bring her father closer.

Kings, princesses, presidents, prime ministers, and representatives of ninety-two countries came to John F. Kennedy's funeral. Millions of grieving U.S. citizens witnessed it too. Many lined the streets of Washington. Others watched on television.

IT'S A FACT!

Jacqueline asked that the same stand that had held Abraham Lincoln's casket be used for her husband's casket. Lincoln had been assassinated in 1865. Other crossovers linked these two murdered presidents. For example, Lincoln's secretary was named Kennedy. Kennedy's secretary was named Lincoln. Both presidents had a man named Johnson succeed them in office.

Caroline reaches up to touch her father's casket.

Jacqueline held the hands of John Jr. and Caroline as they came out of the church. They stood on the steps. It was November 25, 1963, John Jr.'s third birthday. As the casket passed by, the little boy gravely put his hand to his head and saluted his dead father.

Jacqueline Kennedy walked the mile or so from the church to Arlington National Cemetery, where Jack was to be buried. Robert Kennedy was beside her. Many of those attending followed her. Cardinal Cushing, who had married the couple, gave the last blessing for the dead. Just as the cardinal finished his prayer, fifty jet fighter planes

OLD TRADITION

As part of the traditional funeral for a U.S. president, a black horse without a rider is brought forward. The horse has a sword dangling at its side. The stirrups (footholds) hang backward from the saddle. These symbols mean that the rider will never again go into battle. The horse trots beside the caisson (a two-wheeled cart) with the body of the fallen leader in the casket. Six gray horses pull the caisson.

zoomed overhead. Soldiers fired twenty-one shots from cannons. Taps—the music for ending a funeral or other event—sounded over the grave. All of these activities were to honor the dead president. Soldiers removed the flag that covered the casket. They folded it and placed it in Jacqueline's hands. As a final honor, Jacqueline lit an eternal flame over the grave.

Soon after the assassination, the Texas School Book Depository was swarming with police and Secret Service men. A fifteen-year-old boy had told a police officer that he'd seen something sticking out of the building's sixth-floor window as the presidential motorcade passed by. After a roll call of employees, only one person was missing. He was Lee Harvey Oswald, a shipping clerk. Oswald was a loner and an ex-marine with Communist ideals. A call was sent out to all police stations.

Oswald was arrested for the murder of John Kennedy. He claimed he was innocent, but evidence pointed to his guilt. Yet Oswald never had his day in court. On November 24, he was being transferred into a high-security jail. Suddenly, a man later identified as Jack Ruby jumped out of the crowd and shot Oswald in the stomach. He died in the same hospital where President Kennedy had died two days before. Ruby was arrested and stood

Lee Harvey Oswald

trial in Dallas. He was found guilty and was
sentenced to hang. He asked the court to review
the sentence. (He died in jail on January 3, 1967,
while awaiting a new trial.)

President Lyndon Johnson set up a fact-finding
group under the direction of Chief Justice Earl
Warren. After ten months, the Warren Report said
that Oswald was the only assassin of President
Kennedy. Some people felt then and still feel that
John Kennedy's assassination was the result of a
group effort. It's likely that the public will never
know the truth.

AFTERMATH

Laughter was very much a part of the spirit of John
Kennedy. He had a joyfulness and a zest for living
that no amount of pain could weaken. The ability
to laugh at himself was a huge part of his charm.
He took the world and its problems very seriously
but never himself.

A sense of urgency ran through all of his
actions. It was as if the tasks he had set for himself
could only be done by working at full speed. Time,
it seemed, was short. He was the first president to
be born in the twentieth century. And he was very

much a person of his time. He was restless and had a thirst for knowledge. He was deeply committed, not only to the people of the United States but to the peoples of the world. To balance his idealism, he had a logical mind, which let him look at problems clearly. And then he could focus the full power of his mind on solving them.

Some critics have said that John Kennedy's presidency lacked greatness. Yet he fought for many things. These things included stronger civil rights laws and better conditions for the poor, the very old, and the very young. He wanted the peoples of the world to understand one another better. Some of these goals came closer to happening because of John Kennedy. He set things in motion. He moved the world in the direction of peace and cooperation. Nothing about John Kennedy's goals was small. His dreams and his hopes were big. He wasn't afraid of using new ideas to achieve them. His courage was huge. His memory casts a long shadow. It still inspires people to think big and dream large.

GLOSSARY

Addison's disease: an illness that, if not treated, gradually destroys parts of the body that make necessary hormones. People with the disease typically lose weight and are tired.

Berlin Wall: built in 1961, the concrete wall that divided East and West Berlin. It prevented the escape of Germans from Communist East Germany. The wall was taken down in November 1989 after the East German government fell apart.

Democratic Party: one of the two major political parties in the United States. Kennedy belonged to the Democratic Party. The other major party is the Republican Party.

desegregation: stopping the practice of separating people according to age, race, gender, or other factors

developmentally delayed: a way to describe a person who has an ongoing, major delay in the development of skills in many areas, such as language skills, social skills, or thinking skills

Great Depression: lasting from about 1929 to 1942, a period of economic hardship in the United States and throughout the world

Nazi Germany: the name given to Germany from 1933 to 1945, when it was ruled by the Nazi Party

nuclear test: an experiment that involves setting off a nuclear weapon. The nations that signed the 1963 Nuclear Test Ban Treaty agreed to stop testing nuclear weapons in the atmosphere, underwater, or in outer space. The treaty permitted underground tests. A later treaty—signed in 1996— stopped all nuclear testing among those nations that signed.

Peace Corps: a now independent U.S. agency whose U.S. volunteers help people in developing countries improve the way they live

prejudice: an opinion formed unfairly about a certain group

Republican Party: one of the two major political parties in the United States. The Democratic Party, Kennedy's party, is the other.

Senate Foreign Relations Committee: a group of senators who have a say in how the United States deals with other countries

United Nations: an international organization formed in 1945 to keep peace among the nations of the world

World War II: an international conflict that took place in Europe, Asia, and Africa from 1939 through 1945

SOURCE NOTES

26 Geoffrey Perret, *Jack: A Life Like No Other* (New York: Random House, 2001), 111.

26 Ibid.

31 Nigel Hamilton, *JFK: Reckless Youth* (New York: Random House, 1992), 591.

51 Peter Collier and David Horowitz, *The Kennedys: An American Drama* (New York: Summit Books, 1984), 237–238.

52 Ibid.

58 Jacques Lowe, *Portrait: The Emergence of John F. Kennedy* (New York: McGraw Hill Book Co., 1961), 168.

60 "Flashback 1960: Kennedy Beats Nixon," *BBC News*, 2000, http://news.bbc.co.uk/1/hi/world/americas/1015074.stm (December 17, 2003).

60 Lowe, 168.

64 John F. Kennedy, "Inaugural Address, January 20, 1961," *John F. Kennedy Library and Museum*, 2002, http://www.jfklibrary.org/j012061.htm (August 5, 2003).

71 John F. Kennedy, "Radio and Television Report to the American People on Civil Rights," *John F. Kennedy Library and Museum*, 2002, http://www.jfklibrary.org/j061163.htm (August 5, 2003).

83 "The Cold War: A CNN Perspectives Series," *CNN Interactive*, 1999, http://www.cnn.com/SPECIALS/cold.war/episodes/10/script.html (August 5, 2003).

85 John F. Kennedy, "Remarks in the Rudolph Wilde Platz," *John F. Kennedy Library and Museum*, June 26, 1963, http://www/jfklibrary.org/j062663.htm (August 5, 2003).

86 Theodore C. Sorensen, *Kennedy* (New York: Harper and Row, 1965), 582.

87 Martin Luther King Jr., "I Have a Dream," *Holidays on the Net*, 2003, http://www.holidays.net.mlk/speech.htm (August 5, 2003).

88 John F. Kennedy, "Radio and Television Address to the American People on the Nuclear Test Ban Treaty," *John F. Kennedy Library and Museum*, 2002, http://www.jfklibrary.org/jfk_test_ban_speech.html (August 5, 2003).

89 Max Cleland, "Remarks by Senator Max Cleland on the Comprehensive Test Ban Treaty," *Council for a Livable World*, October 13, 1999, http://www.clw.org/pub/clw/coalition/cleland101399.htm (August 5, 2003).

94 "The Hours Before Dallas: A Recollection by President Kennedy's Fort Worth Advance Man." *U.S. National Archives and Records Administration*, 2000, http://www.archives.gov/publications/prologue/summer_2000_jfk_last_day_3.html (August 5, 2003).

96 Perret, 398.

SELECTED BIBLIOGRAPHY

Adler, Bill, ed. *The Kennedy Wit*. New York: Citadel Press, 1964.

Binder, Otto O. *Victory in Space*. New York: Walker and Co., 1962.

Bishop, Jim. *A Day in the Life of President Kennedy*. New York: Random House, 1962.

Burns, James MacGregor. *John Kennedy: A Political Profile*. New York: Harcourt, Brace and Co., 1959.

Collier, Peter, and David Horowitz. *The Kennedys: An American Drama*. New York: Summit Books, 1984.

Donovan, Robert J. *PT 109*. New York: McGraw Hill, 1961.

Heller, Deane, and David Heller. *Jacqueline Kennedy*. Derby, CT: Monarch Book, 1963.

Johnson, Haynes. *The Bay of Pigs*. New York: W. W. Norton, 1964.

Kennedy, John F. *Profiles in Courage*. New York: Harper and Row, 1956.

Kennedy, Robert F. *Thirteen Days*. New York: Signet, New American Library, Inc., 1969.

Lee, Bruce. *Boys' Life of J.F.K.* New York: Sterling, 1961.

Lowe, Jacques. *Portrait: The Emergence of John F. Kennedy*. New York: McGraw Hill Book Co., 1961.

Manchester, William. *Portrait of a President*. Boston: Little, Brown, 1962.

Markmann, Charles L., and Mark Sherwin. *John F. Kennedy: A Sense of Purpose*. New York: St. Martin's Press, 1961.

Martin, Ralph G. *A Hero for Our Times*. New York: MacMillan, 1980.

McCarthy, Joe. *The Remarkable Kennedys*. New York: Dial Press, 1961.

Opotowsky, Stan. *The Kennedy Government*. New York: E. P. Dutton, 1961.

Schlesinger, Arthur M., Jr. *A Thousand Days*. New York: Houghton Mifflin, 1965.

Schoor, Gene. *Young John Kennedy*. New York: Harcourt Brace & World, 1963.

Seaborg, Glenn T. *Kennedy, Khrushchev, and the Test Ban Treaty*. Los Angeles: University of California Press,1981.

Sorensen, Theodore C. *Kennedy*. New York: Harper and Row, 1965.

Tanzer, Lester, ed. *The Kennedy Circle*. Washington, DC: Robert B. Luce, Inc., 1961.

Whalen, Richard. *The Founding Father*. New York: NAL-World, 1964.

FURTHER READING AND WEBSITES

Falkof, Lucille. *John F. Kennedy*. Ada, OK: Garrett Educational Corporation, 1988.

Inside the White House
http://www.pbs.org/weta/whitehouse/whhome.htm
Visitors to this website can explore the White House and even be president!

The John F. Kennedy Library
http://www.jfklibrary.org
This website features pictures of Jack and his family, speeches by him, Jack's biography, and more. It also lists news about upcoming exhibits at the library.

Kennedy, John F. *Why England Slept*. New York: Doubleday, 1961.

Landau, Elaine. *The President's Work: A Look at the Executive Branch.* Minneapolis: Lerner Publications Company, 2004.

Randall, Marta. *John F. Kennedy.* New York: Chelsea House, 1988.

Selfridge, John W. *John F. Kennedy: Courage in Crisis.* New York: Fawcett Columbine, 1989.

White, Theodore H. *The Making of the President 1960.* New York: Atheneum, 1961.

The White House: John Kennedy
http://www.whitehouse.gov/history/presidents/jk35.html
This website offers biographies, portraits, and more on all U.S. presidents.

INDEX

Photo Acknowledgments

The images in this book are used with permission of: The John F. Kennedy Library, pp. 4, 9 [PL-8], 23, 24 [PK 100], 32 [F298], 42 [PX 65-25:21], 50, 58, 67 [AR 7405 D]; 82 [KN-21219], 86 [ST-C232-4-63], 93 [KN-C19364], 95 [STC420-13-63], 100 [AR 8255-12]; © Hulton-Deutsch Collection/CORBIS, p. 6; © CORBIS, p. 11, 102; Library of Congress, pp. 21 (LC-USZ62-16555), 57, 91; Laura Westlund, p. 30; National Archives, pp. 36, 37, 59; © Bettmann/CORBIS, pp. 40, 48, 69, 72; The New Bedford Standard-Times, p. 43; © Marty Nordstrom Photo, Minnesota Historical Society [CZ36.2], p. 55; Office of the Senator, p. 63; © Photo by: The Birmingham News, 2005, p. 70; © Hulton Archive/Getty Images, p. 75; Courtesy of the U.S. Air Force Museum, p. 76; Defense Nuclear Agency, p. 89; © The Everett Collection, p. 96.

Front Cover: The John F. Kennedy Library.